LIGHT PIANO CLASSICS

THE LIBRARY OF
LIGHT PIANO CLASSICS

To Sam Erde—we will love you always

EDITOR: AMY APPLEBY
EDITORIAL ASSISTANT: ELAINE ADAM
MUSIC RESTORATION AND ENGRAVING: ANNE DENVIR

ORDER NO. AM 980661
US INTERNATIONAL STANDARD BOOK NUMBER: 0.8256.2963.2
UK INTERNATIONAL STANDARD BOOK NUMBER: 1.84449.631.7

EXCLUSIVE DISTRIBUTORS:
MUSIC SALES CORPORATION
257 PARK AVENUE SOUTH, NEW YORK, NY 10010 USA
MUSIC SALES LIMITED
8/9 FRITH STREET, LONDON W1D 3JB ENGLAND
MUSIC SALES PTY. LIMITED
120 ROTHSCHILD STREET, ROSEBERY, SYDNEY, NSW 2018, AUSTRALIA

PRINTED IN THE UNITED STATES OF AMERICA BY
VICKS LITHOGRAPH AND PRINTING CORPORATION

AMSCO PUBLICATIONS
A PART OF THE MUSIC SALES GROUP
NEW YORK/LONDON/PARIS/SYDNEY/COPENHAGEN/BERLIN/TOKYO/MADRID

Contents

Tango

Isaac Albéniz
(1860–1909)

Andantino

Minuet

Luigi Boccherini
(1743–1805)

Moderato

una corda
pp un poco animato

TRIO

Polovtsian Dance

from *Prince Igor*

Alexander Borodin
(1833–1887)

Moderato con espressione

Canzonetta

César Cui
(1835–1918)

Allegretto

Love's Dream After the Ball

Alphons Czibilka
(1842–1894)

Moderato

16

Andante amoroso
(The Vision)

The Girl with the Flaxen Hair

Claude Debussy
(1862–1918)

Très calme et doucement expressif

Cédez _ _ // Mouv^t (sans lourdeur)

très doux

Cédez _ // au Mouv^t

Murmuré et en retenant peu à peu

perdendosi ------ *pp*

The Little Negro

Claude Debussy
(1862–1918)

Allegro giusto

Reverie

Claude Debussy
(1862–1918)

Andantino sognando

Pizzicati

from *Sylvia*

Léo Delibes
(1836–1891)

Valse Lente

from *Coppélia*

Léo Delibes
(1836–1891)

Moderato

Entry of the Gladiators

Julius Fucik
(1872–1916)

Moderato

Humoresque

Op. 101, No. 7

Antonín Dvořák
(1841–1904)

Poco lento e gracioso

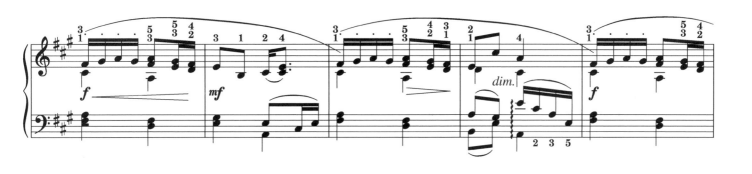

Silhouette

Antonín Dvořák
(1841–1904)

Andantino

The Golden Wedding

Gabriel-Marie

Allegretto

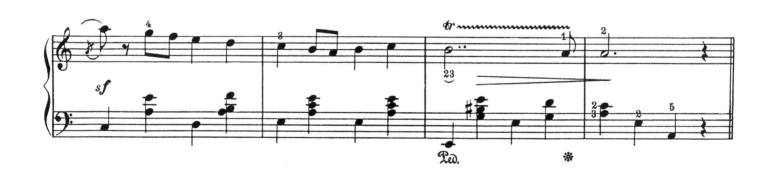

The Secret

Leonard Gautier

Allegretto con moto

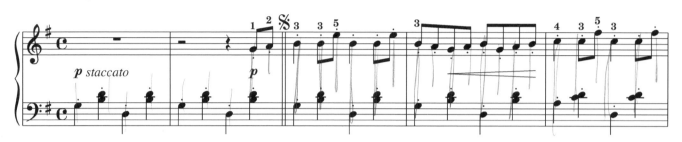

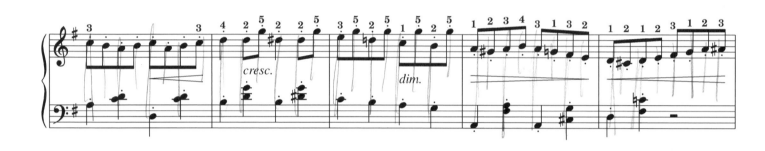

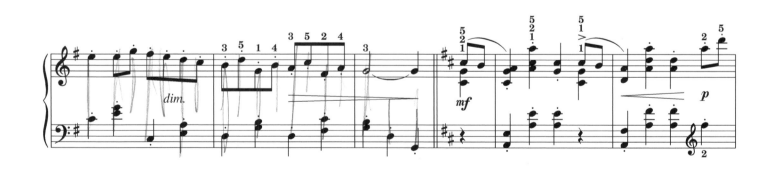

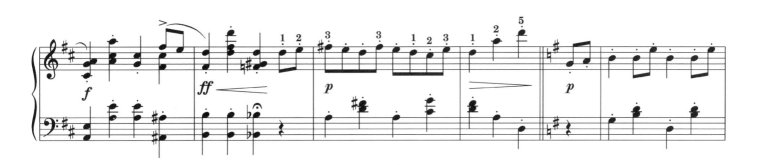

Amaryllis

Joseph Ghys
(1801–1848)

Allegro moderato

Gavotte

François Gossec
(1734–1829)

Allegretto

51

The Dying Poet

Louis Moreau Gottschalk
(1829–1869)

Andante

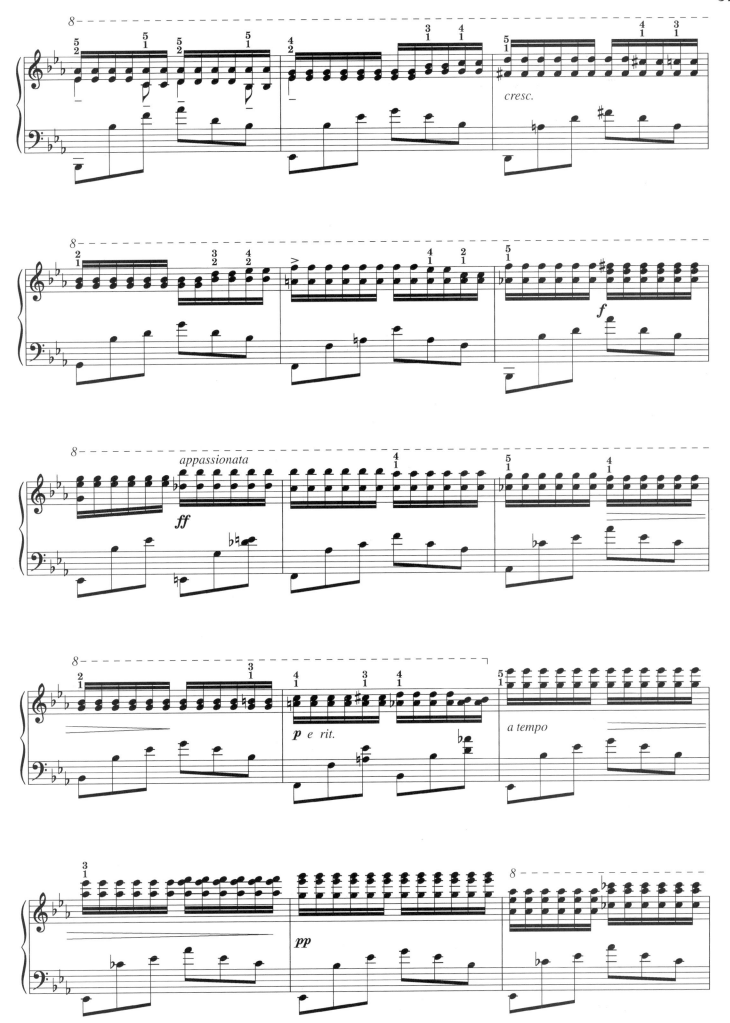

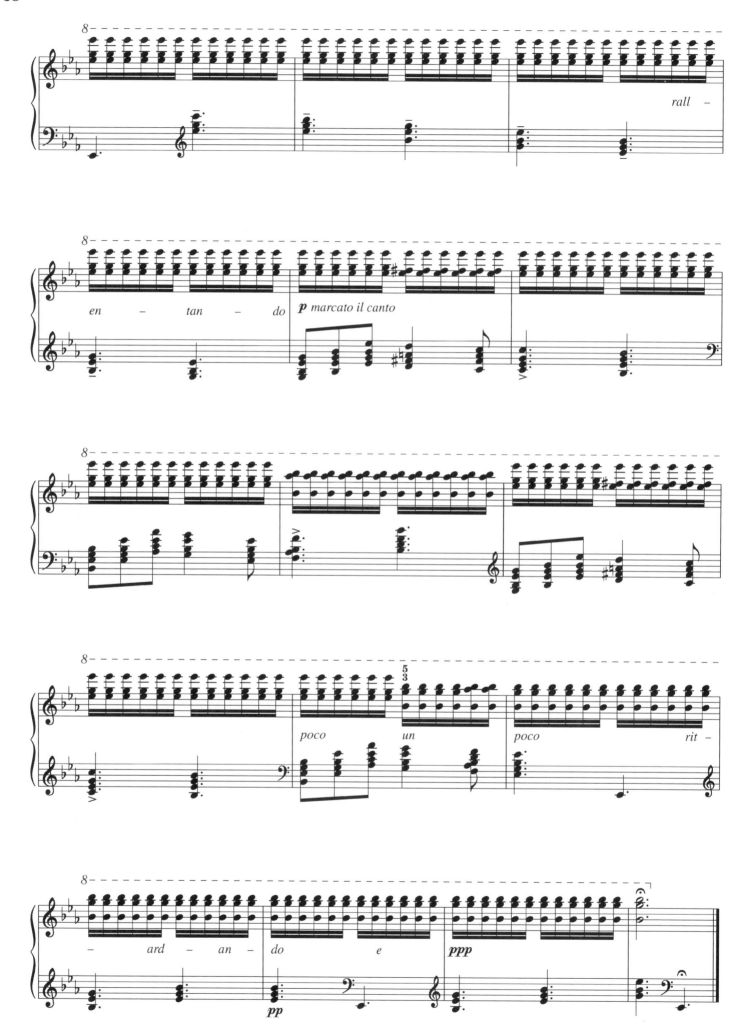

Papillon

Op. 43, No 1

Edvard Grieg
(1843–1907)

Allegro grazioso

Funeral March of a Marionette

Charles Gounod
(1818–1893)

Playera

Enrique Granados
(1867–1916)

Andantino quasi allegretto

Norwegian Dance
Op. 35, No. 2

Edvard Grieg
(1843–1907)

Allegretto tranquillo e grazioso

Canzonetta

Victor Herbert
(1859–1924)

An Alexis

Johann Hummel
(1778–1837)

Key of G

Andantino espressivo

Longing

5/2

Halfdan Kjerulf
(1815–1868)

Andantino espressivo

Waves of the Danube

Iosif Ivanovici
(c.1845–1902)

Con moto

Flower Song

Gustav Lange
(1830–1889)

Lento moderato

Thine Own

Gustav Lange
(1830–1889)

Andante espressione

Liebestraum

Franz Liszt
(1811–1886)

Poco allegro, con affetto

dolce cantando

poco cresc. e agitato

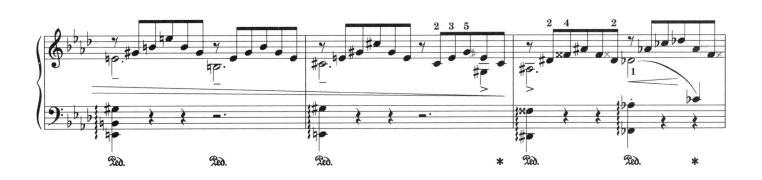

cresc. robusto

poco a poco riten.

At Sunset

Edward MacDowell
(1861–1908)

Allegro con gajezza

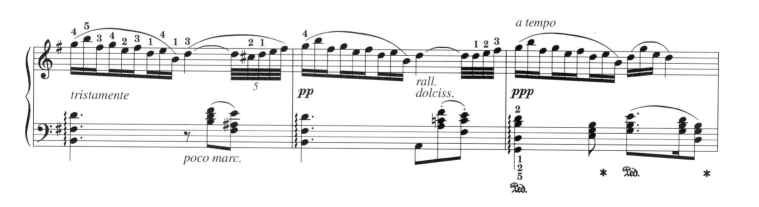

Intermezzo

Op. 39, No. 9

Edward MacDowell
(1861–1908)

Allegretto

To the Moonlight

Op. 28, No. 3

Edward MacDowell
(1861–1908)

With breadth and tenderness

Dance of the Clowns

from *A Midsummer Night's Dream*

Felix Mendelssohn
(1809–1847)

Spring Song

Felix Mendelssohn
(1809–1847)

Allegretto grazioso

Narcissus

Ethelbert Nevin
(1862–1901)

Andante con moto

The Marriage of Figaro

Themes

Wolfgang Amadeus Mozart
(1756–1791)

Allegro moderato (Sweet Ladies)

Tempo di Marcia (Wedding March)

Apache Dance

Jacques Offenbach
(1819–1880)

118

Can Can

from *Orpheus*

Jacques Offenbach
(1819–1880)

Allegro

Tales of Hoffman

Themes

Jacques Offenbach
(1819–1880)

Moderato

Rather slowly (Barcarolle, "Beautiful Night of Love")

128

Dance of the Hours

Amilcare Ponchielli
(1834–1886)

Moderato

Over the Waves

Juventino Rosas

Legato

Flight of the Bumblebee

Nikolai Rimsky-Korsakov
(1844–1908)

The Young Prince and Princess

from *Scheherezade*

Nikolai Rimsky-Korsakov
(1844–1908)

Allegretto

with Pedal

Melody in F

Anton Rubinstein
(1829–1894)

142

Romance

Anton Rubinstein
(1829–1894)

Andante con moto

The Swan

Camille Saint-Saëns
(1835–1921)

Adagio e legato

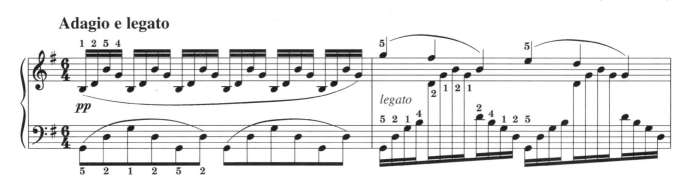

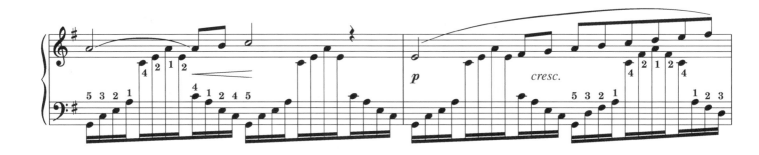

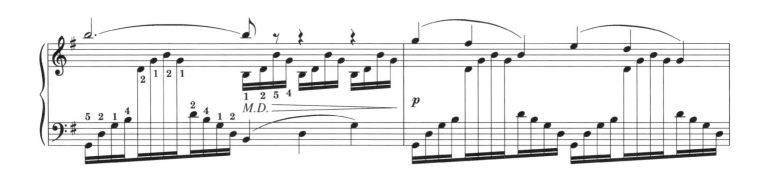

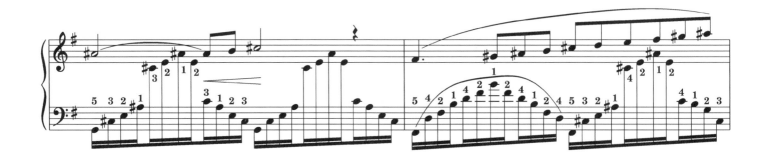

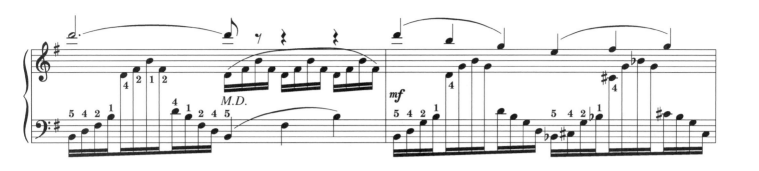

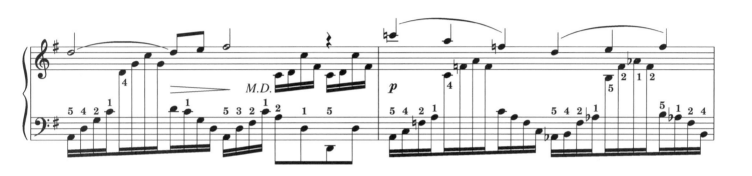

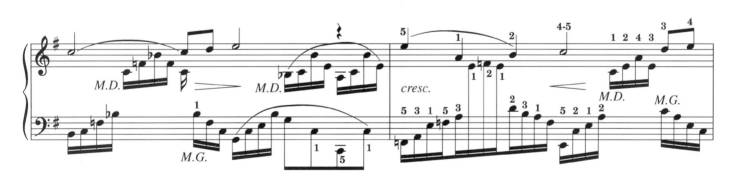

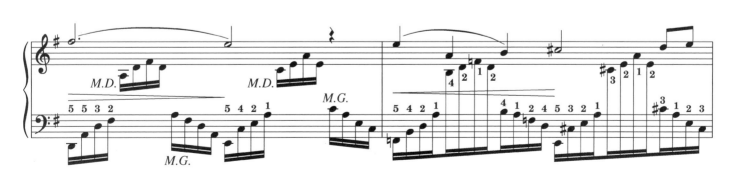

Entr'acte

from *Rosamunde*

Franz Schubert
(1797–1828)

Andantino

150

MINORE

Moment Musicale

Franz Schubert
(1797–1828)

Allegro moderato

Three Waltzes

Franz Schubert
(1797–1828)

Allegro moderato

№ 1

№ 2

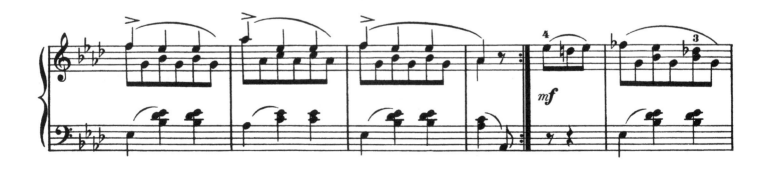

Slumber Song

Robert Schumann
(1810–1856)

Allegretto

The Happy Farmer

Robert Schumann
(1810–1856)

Allegretto

Remembrance

Robert Schumann
(1810–1856)

Espressivo

Traumerei

Robert Schumann
(1810–1856)

Moderato

The Wild Horseman

Robert Schumann
(1810–1856)

Allegro con brio

Album Leaf

Alexander Scriabin
(1872–1915)

Andante piacevole

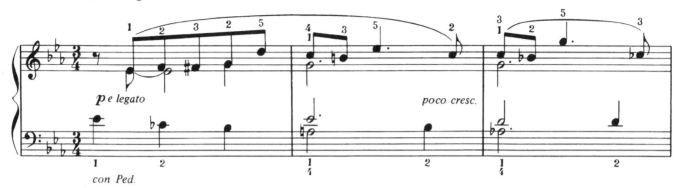

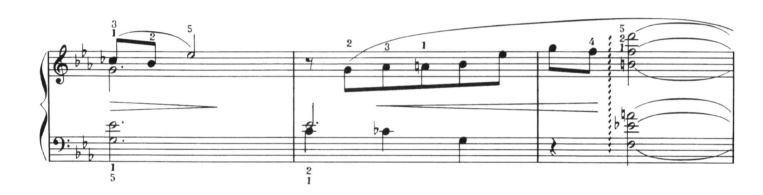

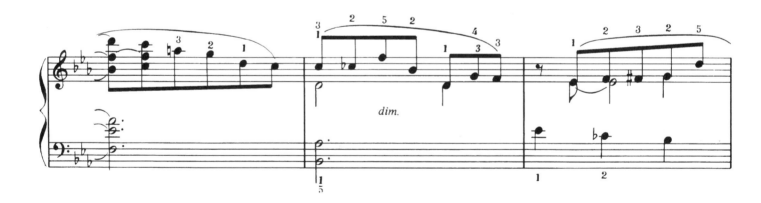

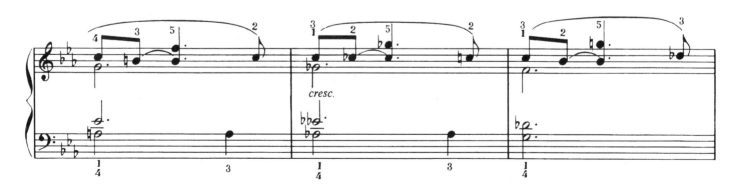

El Capitan

John Philip Sousa
(1854–1932)

Moderato con moto

The Stars and Stripes Forever

John Philip Sousa
(1854–1932)

Energetico

Die Fledermaus

Themes

Johann Strauss II
(1825–1899)

Moderato con moto (*Such a Fine Gentleman*)

con Ped. ad lib.

poco string.

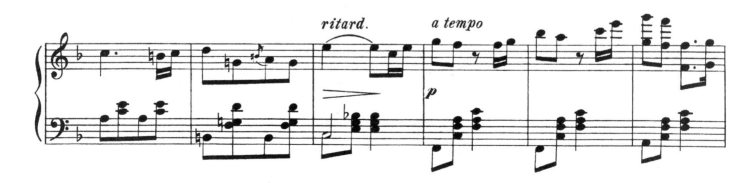

ritard.

a tempo

Allegretto *(Waltz)*

174

(Ah, What a Feast, What a Night of Joy)

The Beautiful Blue Danube

Johann Strauss II
(1825–1899)

Legato

One Heart, One Mind

Johann Strauss II
(1825–1899)

INTRODUCTION

Moderato

Tempo di mazurka

Pizzicato Polka

Johann Strauss II
(1825–1899)

D.C. ⊕ to Coda.

Più Allegro

Coda

Tales from the Vienna Woods

Johann Strauss II
(1825–1899)

Allegro moderato

H.M.S. Pinafore

Themes

Arthur Sullivan
(1842–1900)

Allegro ("We Sail the Ocean Blue")

Allegretto ("I'm Called Little Buttercup")

192

Allegretto ("I Am the Captain of the *Pinafore*")

Maestoso ("For He Is an Englishman")

The Mikado

Themes

Arthur Sullivan
(1842–1900)

Allegro ("The Flowers That Bloom in the Spring")

196

Allegretto grazioso ("Three Little Maids from School")

Con Ped. ad lib.

Patience

Themes

Arthur Sullivan
(1842–1900)

Allegretto

(A magnet hung in a hardware shop)

Allegro Vivace

(So go to him and say to him)

Pirates Chorus

from *Pirates of Penzance*

Arthur Sullivan
(1842–1900)

Moderato

Light Cavalry

Themes

Franz von Suppé
(1820–1895)

Allegro (Overture)

Andantino con moto (Czardas)

Romeo and Juliet

(Theme)

Peter Ilyich Tchaikovsky
(1840–1893)

Moderato espressivo

Swan Lake

(Theme)

Peter Ilyich Tchaikovsky
(1840–1893)

Andante

Dance of the Sugar Plum Fairy

from *The Nutcracker*

Peter Ilyich Tchaikovsky
(1840–1893)

Andante non troppo

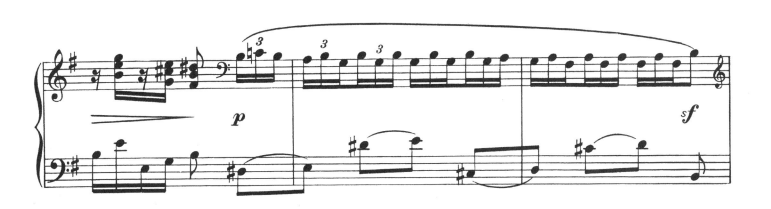

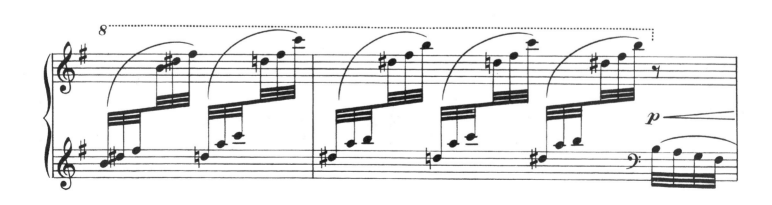

Sweet Dreams

Peter Ilyich Tchaikovsky
(1840–1893)

Legato

Waltz

from *Serenade for Strings*

Peter Ilyich Tchaikovsky
(1840–1893)

Legato

Under the Double Eagle

Josef Franz Wagner
(1856–1908)

Simple Aveu

François Thomé
(1850–1909)

Moderato et legato

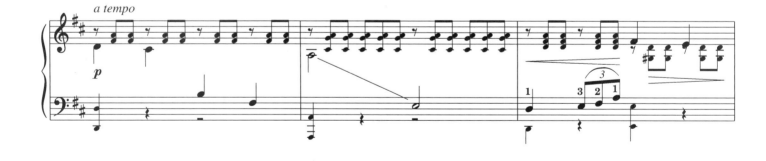

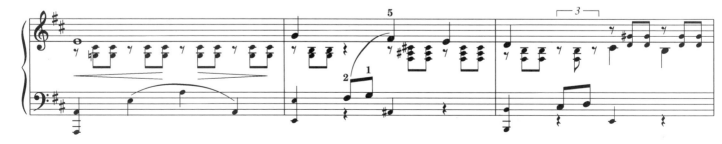

226

227

My Dream

Emil Waldteufel
(1837–1915)

Allegretto

D.C. al 3.

4.

Skaters Waltz

Emil Waldteufel
(1837–1915)

Moderato

D.C.al Fine

The Dove

(*La Paloma*)

Sebastian Yradier
(1809–1885)

Index